The Beauty in the Pursuit of God

"On the Road to Wholeness"

Shareka Marbra

Dedication

iii

This book is dedicated to all those who may still be dealing with past hurts and have yet allowed the Lord to heal you. I'm sorry that in life you may have had to endure some horrible things, but I promise you that there is a God, and his name is Jesus who can turn all those things around for your good if you let him. Your test was only a message to help free someone else. You are an overcomer through Christ Jesus so be free in the name of Jesus.

And we know that all things work together for the good to them that love God, to them who are called according to his purpose.

Roman 8:28

I'm rooting for you!

Acknowledgment

For God hath not given us the spirit of fear; but of power, and of love, and of a sound mind.

2 Timothy 1:7

Thank you, God, for empowering me with your holy boldness to release my life's testimony that could break generational curses and allow others to come forth out of bondage. Freedom is our portion and who the Son sets free is free indeed. All glory belongs to you only. Amen.

Contents

Chapter 1

Loneliness

As a child, some may vaguely remember what it was like growing up in a home where there was a sense of happiness, a sense of peace, a sense of unity, or a sense of love. But to tell you the truth, from what I remember, my life's journey started out with a sense of uncertainty and loneliness. I know what you are thinking, "My goodness, you were too young to even comprehend those types of feelings." But guess what I did, and at that early age I now realize that God was molding me then into who I am today.

You see, no one knows what the journey ahead entails, and no one knows what the outcome consists of. All I knew was to keep moving forward and hope for better days. I was not the only child. I had one older brother and one younger sister at that appointed time in my life. I loved my family, and I knew that they loved me too but sometimes family had a funny way of showing it because they did not experience the kind of love that they hoped for growing up as a child themselves.

You see, my mom had me and my siblings at an incredibly early age, and now that I am an adult, I understand that she was just a baby trying to raise babies. Because, like me her reason for having us was because she wanted to feel loved. Look how that same cycle can travel through generations without anyone ever noticing. What a shame, but thank God, he loved me enough to free me from that pain.

Growing up in a household where there were multiple families was a joy at times, but it was no picnic in the ballpark either. There were family gatherings one day, and in that same breath, somebody was getting a beating put on them. I can distinctly hear the music playing those Oldies but Goodies jams while the whole community joined in to bust a move. So much laughter filled the air as I watched through the window seal because kids did not have any place in grown folks' business. But occasionally, you have that one uncle or dad that would come in the room where you were and give you a swig of beer, "Talking about it will kill the worms." Worms! What worms?! And from that day forward I never took a sip of beer again.

Just think about it. From a child's perspective, that statement scared me half to death. Who in their right mind would want to experience a horror story like that? But the night was young, and they partied all night long. When we arose the next morning, we would find Daddy in the kitchen cooking breakfast for what seemed like the whole neighborhood because some folks just did not make it home. They were either too tired to drive or plain old drunk. But again, the multitude of people there somehow made me feel invisible. All I wanted was to be noticed somehow somewhere instead of feelings of loneliness.

It came a time when Mom and dad were no longer a couple anymore, so we went to Grandma's house to live instead. Now, here we go again. There was so much family at Grandma's house every day that you would have thought that multiple family members lived there, too. On top of the family being there, we were crammed in a three-bedroom house, sharing bedrooms, sometimes sleeping on pallets on the floor, and using furniture as a resting place, too.

Do not get me wrong, I am grateful for family, but my insides were screaming bloody Mary because for once in my lifetime, I just wanted to feel loved like you see in the hallmark movies where the families seem perfectly happy and functional. Even though we lived in those conditions, our needs were always taken care of. My mother was a hard-working woman who always worked to provide for us, and my dad was here and there. But one thing I know is my dad was a jack of all trades. That man knew how to do everything you could think of.

From cooking to cleaning to mechanical work and inventing all kinds of riding gadgets. Grandma was always cooking and filling up her home with people we never knew, but she could do whatever she wanted because it was her house that we lived in. I can remember people coming and going out of grandma's house with plates of food and sometimes they would even take time, sit down at the dinner table, and listen as she told them stories about the Lord. Those people knew that they were always welcome at Grandma's house because she cared just as much for them as she did for us. Grandma was a God-fearing woman who loved the Lord with all her heart, and she loved to sing praises to him.

Every morning, she would be up cooking, singing her gospel music, and smoking her cigarettes. Sometimes, grandma would be busy doing multiple things, and she would let me light her cigarette on the stove or in the toaster, and I would be in heaven thinking I was grown while taking a couple of puffs here or there, but eventually, she would catch me because the ashes were so far back that she just knew it didn't get to hang on its own. But still, to my surprise, none of that took away the feelings that were beginning to possess me.

As time proceeded to pass by, I began to find comfort in one of my elementary school teachers. Even though there was a classroom full of students, she treated me like I was her very own. She paid special attention to me until, eventually, she became a safe place for me. I was excited to go to school, not too much to learn but because I felt loved. She did not have any children of her own at that time, so I guess you can say that I was her daughter in some sense. She always encouraged me to be better and do my best no matter what task was handed to me. I can recall her husband and herself showing up at the house one day to take me to Disney World.

As I lay outside on my blanket with anticipation, her car pulled up, and oh, what joy did I feel for someone to spend some alone time with just me. That was one of the happiest days of my life as a child. I remember before she took a job elsewhere, she made me promise her that I would finish school before I decided to have children. And guess what? That promise was mine to keep because I had my first child after I graduated from high school. You know God sometimes places people in your pathway because he knows exactly what you need in that very moment, and I am grateful for that.

The next year, she was long gone, and now I was back in a place wondering how the next events in my life would turn out. I was so accustomed to feelings of numbness that I began to live a fantasy life inside of my head. No one even knew the thoughts that went through my mind because everyone was so busy existing. By this time, Mom had already met a new man. We moved out of grandma's house into our own and all hell broke loose. My world was turned upside down, and feelings of isolation began to creep in. Some days, what seemed less than others, we were portrayed to the world as a loving family. Do not get me wrong, we did all sorts of things as a family, including a lot of family outings, but deep down inside, I did not feel like I belonged there.

Two new siblings popped up in the picture, and the cycle continued. Of course, Mom had married this man, but I was too young to remember how that even played out. Now it is five of us and here is where I learn how to be a caretaker. My mom always told me that when she had my sister after me, I was her little helper, but I was too young to remember that. But with these two bouncing baby girls, I had the pleasure of helping mommy raise them.

As they grew into the toddler stage, I was already comforting them like they were my own. I loved my sisters even though they were a little spoiled, all three of them, but nothing could pull me away from them because a sense of love was always present. There were fun times that I can remember when my brother and I would pull all the pillows from the couch, put them on the floor, and toss our younger siblings back in forth in the air. Do not worry, the pillows were there to protect them as they sometimes slipped through our fingers.

It was not until they got a little older that those same feelings began to resurface again. Even though all the attention was on them already, it really shifted to them because their biological father was in the home. It went from trying to fit in, to being pushed to the back burner. At least, that is what it felt like to me. Because I was not his biological daughter and did not call him dad, it seemed like rage was always present.

Do you know how it feels as a child to try to make someone love you without getting on their bad side? It was the worst feeling ever. I was so terrified, so I tried to do everything right so that I did not get yelled at or get a whopping. I longed for my dad to come to rescue me, but his lack of being present sent me into a depression. The house was always filled with people from families on both sides, big and small to adult friends of my stepdad.

While mom was working, he was left to tend to us, but somehow, most of the time, I always ended up in my room while all the children were able to go outside and play or ended up helping prepare the food. I could never understand what I did to deserve such a harsh punishment. It felt like I was drifting away, and nothing made sense anymore. At night, I would be terrified to go to sleep because it always seemed as if someone were watching me.

One night, a hand touches my private parts, and as I jump to discover if anyone is there, to my surprise, I see the body of someone lying on the floor of my bedroom. I was so afraid I did not know what was going on. I was only a child, but my heart told me it was wrong. So, I kept my mouth closed until one day, that person approached me, took me outside on the porch, and said to me, "You know there are some things you cannot tell your momma. It will break her heart." And at that moment a sense of sadness began to come over me. I mean, I did not want to break my momma's heart, but I did not want to continue to feel unsafe, either.

There were so many men coming in and out of our house that I began to look at every one of them with disgust. How did I end up in a situation as a child that could tear relationships up? Well, eventually, I mustarded up courage, walked into my mom's room, and laid it on her. I told her exactly what happened, and she did not believe me, and my little heart was crushed. From that moment on all the hope of love that I envisioned went right out the window. The only sense of security I felt was when my cousins visited our home, and I just knew that someone would rescue me.

If you have not noticed yet, I was not a child who was raised in church. But back then, the church mothers in the community would pick up children and carry them to church. If parents did not go, children surely did not have a choice in the matter. When it was time for church, we had to be ready and wait outside for someone to come pick us up. I can remember our trips on the way to church. We would pack together like some Vienna sausages.

All the children would be seated together in the back row in the pews, making lots of noise, and all you could see was the mothers of the church pointing fingers and lip-talking like we understood what they were saying. It was funny because even though we did not hear them, we knew exactly what they meant. Occasionally, one of the mothers would have to come to sit by us, and if we kept that foolishness up, our ears would be on fire, or some unrecognizable part of our bodies would be in pain. To keep us quiet, peppermints and candy were always our reward, but eventually, I got tired of eating those things. I

never knew what was going on or why we were even there, but one thing that I loved was to see the choir sing. People would be shouting, dancing, and running around the church like they had lost their minds. It was a sight to see and funny at times, but now I understand that they had some fire shot up in their bones, and that was how they praised God. That was the extent of church for me and that only lasted for a little while, but it was always a joy to get out of the house and be with friends.

My life was not a total disaster. I know that with God there is always purpose in everything that he allows you to go through, but it just seemed like opposition came one after another. The chaos in the house never ended and the effects of it began to show outwardly. Everyone in the house, including mom, was afraid to speak out and voice their opinions for fear of being reprimanded. It was like our every move was controlled and put under a microscope. Even at an early age, we were not allowed to wear clothes that hugged our bodies. I was a little girl my body was not developing rapidly like some do today.

Back then, I never understood why I had to walk around wearing baggy clothes that consumed my body, but as I got older, it all made sense to me. Mom was still submerging herself in work, and I suspected it was because she did not want to be home and deal with the realities of life in our home. Work was a safe place for her where she could get peace of mind. Meanwhile, the house continued to be full of uninvited guests, well, at least, that is who they were in my head.

Chapter 2
Need for Acceptance

As the teenage years began to creep up, Mom and Stepdad started letting me have sleepovers. I was not allowed to stay at anyone's house because I had responsibilities to tend to in our home. Someone had to take care of my siblings while mom was working and stepdad was out doing God knows what. By that time, I had already known how to cook a full-course meal, clean the entire house, drive without an adult present, grocery shop on my own, and take care of my siblings' needs before I hit the age of thirteen.

As the years continued to go by, I found myself trying to find acceptance in the friends that I made at school. I had a few friends that I held dear to my heart from elementary school, but I started to make new friends in middle school and merge their way of living with my sheltered lifestyle. To me, it seemed like they were so free, and they could do whatever they wanted to do, but in the company of my house, it did not go down like that. My friends wore makeup to school tight-fitting clothes, and were even allowed to have boyfriends. At least, that is how it appeared to me. I know their moms would have lost their minds if they knew they had boyfriends at school. Boys began to be on my radar at that time, but all I would hear from them was that I was ugly, too skinny, and gap-toothed.

I was so embarrassed until one day, I started putting paper in between the big gap that I had in the front of my mouth. I remember one boy started calling me yoo-hoo gums because my gums were so black. And that led to some of the other boys starting to call me that, too. What made matters worse was every time an adult who knew my dad would see me, they would always tell me that I looked just like my ugly dad, so I grew up thinking I was ugly. It hurt my feelings so bad, but it did not stop me from wanting to be accepted.

So, I began to hang out with my brother and his friends to try and fit in. My brother did not like that, but truth be told, I felt like they were taking my brother away from me. I was already wearing baggy clothes and playing contact sports with my cousins at home until I grew accustomed to wanting to just be with boys all the time. Some of my girlfriends were cheerleaders, and because of my home situation, I just knew that that would not be acceptable to my parents. So, a tomboy I became. I loved playing sports. I wanted to try out for the football team, but one of my male teachers, who I looked up to as a father figure, would not let me.

He was the football coach, and I was so angry with him because a girl ended up making the team. That was the first time I ever witnessed a girl being able to play a contact sport with boys. Times were changing, but I did not let that stop me from playing sports, so I tried out for the girls' basketball team at school. I was a great athlete. I was super-fast, and I could handle the ball well, which landed me a spot on the team as the point guard. When our season was over, I held the record for the most points ever scored at that school for girls. I was unstoppable.

All that practice and competing against my cousins at home paid off. Even though these activities sometimes took my mind off the problems I dealt with at home, it did not stop them from appearing in other areas of my life. Throughout my time playing basketball in middle school not one time could I look in the stands and see my mom there cheering me on. I longed for her love and support, but I understood that she had to work to provide for us and that is how it was going to be. I was so broken and unsure of myself until I buried my feelings. To the eye of someone else, I looked completely fine, but deep down inside, I was drowning in a sea of emotions.

It did not take long before police officers and people in the community began to look at our home as a drug house. From all the horrible things I experienced in that house, you would have thought we were starring in a Hollywood movie scene. All the extracurricular activities that my stepdad was involved in outside of our home attracted so much attention to our house. I mean, could you imagine being a child and your house getting shot up, and all you could do was jump to the floor, praying no one was injured. Or could you imagine strangers trying to break into your house and you, as a child, having to run to the utility room and arm yourself with weapons? Better yet could you imagine a man coming to your house with a baseball bat to fight your parent while you were just playing outside in the yard.

My experiences were real and unforgettable. I can remember one of my stepdad's drunken friends talking to me and looking at me like I was a piece of meat that he wanted to devour. The next thing I noticed was a beer bottle hitting the man in the face, and an argument transpired. I was so scared I did not know what to do. Then, a few weeks later, my stepdad got shot by the same man he hit in the face with a beer bottle. As I got older, I would hear rumors in the street about my stepdad. At least, that is what I thought they were.

All I could think about at that time was what my mother was going through and how she felt about it all. Those truths were a hard pill to swallow but still life went on. Living there became unbearable for me, so I decided to pack some of my belongings and ran away to my dad's mom's house. After being there for a couple of days, my stepdad and mom tracked me down, came to get me, and put a beating on me that I will never forget. At that time, my dad was living with my grandma, and I wanted to tell him what was going on, but I knew things would have gotten out of control if he had known. So once again, I kept my mouth shut and kept it moving.

The average person might be asking themselves, did she

even get to enjoy her childhood? And my answer would be no. I had to be groomed to take on adult responsibilities instead of enjoying my childhood years as a normal child. There were times when family members were trying to kidnap me so that I could escape all the madness in the home, but when they did, I would be brought right back home to suffer in silence. There seemed to be no hope for me, so I stayed to myself.

By the time my youngest sister was five years old, my stepdad had gotten himself caught up in a world of trouble with the police officers and ended up going to prison for the entire time I was in high school. Whew, what a relief that was for me. I could finally have a little bit of freedom. My dad started popping back in and out of my life, and I was happy to see him even though he was not around for some of the toughest years of my life at that moment. So, off to high school, I went. I was about fifteen years old then and did not like school.

I had no one to encourage me to get an education and become someone people could be proud of, so I did the bare minimum all throughout my time in high school. I was still considered a tomboy, but as time went by, I tried adjusting to wear clothes that fit me and showed my shape, but I was so uncomfortable. Every time someone would give me a compliment about how I looked I would go right back to wearing my loose clothing. I met some great friends who I am still connected to this day but that does not mean that I did not have my share of backstabbers either.

My relationship with my mom began to be restored, but to be honest, I am not even sure that my mom had known that I resented her for a lot of things I endured growing up as a child. My mom became more lenient and allowed me to spend overnights with some of my friends. They had a lot more life experiences than I did. Growing up, I was not allowed to have a boyfriend, let alone have conversations with them over the phone, but that did not stop me from having a crush on a few of them. While in the company of my friends, I attended all kinds of wild parties and nightclub activities. I was not even old enough to be in those types of establishments, but where there is a will, there is a way. I was there.

Still seeking acceptance from people, I ended up trying things like alcoholic beverages that I did not care for and going to places that made my skin crawl, but once I consumed a little bit of alcohol, my awareness was numb to it all. I partied like a rock star. I hated the aftereffects, but I continued to indulge in it. I ended up dating one guy throughout my whole high school years and that ended in devastation. He ended up going off to college because he was older than me, and there, I was still there like a fool trying to continue a relationship that was well over before it ended. I had my share of heartbreaks and broken friendships, but I hated being alone, so I continued to allow myself to go through the motions until we parted ways.

The Beauty in the Pursuit of God

One of the toughest things in high school that I had to deal with was not being able to play the sport that I loved. That is right, you guessed it, basketball. My first year of playing high school basketball was a total catastrophe. I tore my ACL, MCL, and Meniscus all from one injury. I know you do not know what that means, and neither did I, but I knew my basketball-playing days were over.

On top of that, I had pins put in my knee, and I had to go through extensive physical therapy for six months. I am not a person who deals with pain very easily, so it was safe to say that my hopes and dreams of playing basketball in the WNBA were over. But hey, our plans are not always God's plans for us, so I kept it moving. Finally, the day came when it was time for me to graduate. I was so excited because in my head, I was eighteen now, and I was grown, so to me, that meant I could do whatever I wanted to do, but that's not how things went in my house. I still had to help Mom take care of my younger siblings and at that moment, I was fine with that.

Even though I continued my normal responsibilities I began to hang out with some of my guy friends. I found myself increasingly still indulging in things that I hated to do, but all my friends were doing it, and I wanted to look cool, so I did it anyway. Until I found myself in the home of one of my friends who forced himself on me. I was heartbroken. For someone I called my friend to do something horrific like that hurt me to the core. But once again,

I kept my mouth shut and kept it moving. You see, sometimes a person can be going through so much trauma that they become a mastermind at masking their realities. When in their presence, you would never know what they were going through because, through it all, they always showed a smile, put others before them, and loved you past your infirmities. That's the kind of person I was. I love people, and I just wanted to see them happy despite what I was going through.

Chapter 3
Oh Shoot

Shortly after I graduated from high school, I moved in with my grandma, that's right, my mom's mom. I got a job working in a juice factory, which I loved. It was me and a few other women working in an atmosphere with mostly men. My tomboyish instincts kicked back in, and there I found myself working in a position where a woman had never worked before. It was dangerous, and it was a challenge, but who was I to turn down a challenge?

I laugh in the face of challenges. I guess my supervisor had it out for me or something because he would be down my back like sweat dripping on a sunny day at the beach. I was doing an excellent job, but all my coworkers complained to him because they thought it was too dangerous for a woman to be working that palletizer machine. Previously, before I started working there, a man's leg got caught in the machine and was chopped off.

That is the story that was told to me, but I welcomed the challenge. When it comes to doing something that I love, I am going to stick to it and finish the task. I only worked there for a few months because the fumes began to make me nauseated. Oh, shoot, I thought to myself, what could have started that madness. Unbeknownst to me, there was a baby growing inside of me.

It took me by complete surprise, but like my grandma always says, "If you are doing grown-up things, grown-up things are going to happen." Oh, shoot, oh shoot, oh shoot! How was I going to tell my mom, let alone the father of the baby that I was with child, like the old folks say. I was terrified. Me having a baby with someone who I was not even in a relationship with. This is not how I envision my life to be. I thought I would find the man of my dreams. He would sweep me off my feet, and we would get married and live happily ever after. That was a nice thought, but I had to snap back into reality quickly.

During that time, one of my relatives was killed in an armed robbery. It broke my heart because my cousin was a happy person, always looking out for everyone. He was so cool. If you have ever seen the movie Straight Outta Compton, despite what was going on, you would see all the nice old-school cars with rims, loud music playing, and hydraulics just cruising down the street. That was my cousin. He would be leaning so far back in the car that you would have thought the car was driving itself. You could not miss his gigantic smile.

All 32 pearly whites were showing, shining bright like the sun. His death shocked the whole community, especially those who loved him dearly. But once again in my world, you had to learn how to cope with things and keep moving. Now back to this baby that I was carrying. I was not ready to be a mother, let alone raise a child that I could not give back to its rightful owner.

I had done so much of that growing up until, at this point in my life, I was tired of being responsible for others. I just wanted to have fun, travel, and explore the world. Another dream was thrown out the window. My sole purpose for moving with my grandmother was to help care for her. She was getting older, and in her poor health condition, it was starting to become harder for her to do things on her own.

My grandmother was a strong black woman despite everything she endured growing up, from physical abuse, mental abuse, and verbal abuse, you name it. She kept a smile on her face and persevered through her life's challenges. At an early age, my grandma suffered from an aneurysm bursting in her head. Everyone thought that she was going to die, but God had other plans. She went into a coma, and when she came out, she knew the entire Bible. That was her testimony and a great one that was.

At that time, I still did not know who God was. You know you can go through spurts of life hearing about him, but it is not until you have a real encounter with him that a transformation within you begins. It had not happened to me, so there I was, still going through the motions of life. Finally, I decided to tell my mother and the father of the baby that I was pregnant.

They were all excited, but feelings of shame and embarrassment began to overshadow me. I mean, I did not want to be with this man that is the main reason I was not in a relationship with him. My mentality at that time was I was going to do a man just as he did me. What a poor mindset that I was dealing with. Life's struggles can turn you into a person that you do not want to be. As the baby continued to grow inside of me, we eventually became a couple. I was not used to being in a relationship where I had to share the same space with someone. Oh, how I hated it. In the beginning, I felt suffocated, but he grew on me. When it came time for us to have the baby, he was arrested and sent to prison because of some extracurricular activities he was involved in outside of the home, too. Which left me to have our baby in the company of my family.

What a joy it was to finally see my son. I mean, that pregnancy took me through the wringer, and I was even happier that he was not inside of me anymore. During labor, my son was playing hide and seek. He would appear and then go back inside of me. That went on for what seemed like hours until both of our heart rates began to drop, and an emergency C-section had to be performed. I was the last person in my family to see my son. My entire immediate family had taken him a bath, washed his hair, combed his hair, moisturized his body, and dressed him all before I had a chance to come out of the recovery room.

I was so mad, but the support from them all and finally being able to hold my baby was worthwhile. At that time, my grandmother was not doing so great by herself that she had to live in a nursing home for a while. In the process of living with my grandmom I was able to get my own apartment, but I was so afraid of living on my own that I moved back in with my mom, and she helped me take care of my son. I enjoyed taking care of my son and watching him grow up, but I was not the type of person who could sit down for long.

After a few months of being home back to the workforce I went. Fifteen months had breezed by, and the father of my son was back home. While my grandmother was away, my mother and I maintained my grandmother's mortgage so that she could keep her house when it was time for her to come home, but that did not go the way that we planned. Grandma had to stay in the nursing home a little while longer. Even though I had my own apartment, I decided to go back to a familiar place, grandma's house.

My apartment did not go to waste. It was occupied by some friends and relatives of mine. Why not help others when I had a choice where I wanted to stay? So, my son's father moved into my grandmother's house with me. I expected us to be a happy family but that is all they were my expectations. Now, here we go again. There is nothing worse than being in a relationship and feeling all alone.

I practically raised my son on my own. His father was here and there, which brought back feelings of loneliness and thinking I was not good enough to experience a life of love. I did everything in my power to try and make things work, but he had other things on his mind. He went back to the streets but always tracked me. There goes that controlling spirit that I was accustomed to. There was nothing I could do or no place that I could go that this man did not know about.

I was beginning to think that he had spies watching me, yet I did not know what he was involved in out there. Then came the multiple women, the arguments, the drugs, the fights, the verbal, physical, and mental abuse until one day, I tried to escape it all, and a gun was put to my head. The crazy thing about it is I was not crying. I was not afraid of what could have occurred at that moment. The only words that came out of my mouth were, "If you are going to shoot me, shoot me because God is the only one who determines if I live or die," and the strangest thing happened. He put the gun down and began to weep.

All this went on right in the company of one of his relatives. You never know what type of state of mind someone has until things do not go their way. His family members were so terrified, but my faith in that very moment that I did not know I had rested on God's plan. What you think is love is really not love. We've been so groomed by our environment that these things have become a norm for us. I thought that I could help this man and encourage him to change his life when, in actuality, I was losing myself.

That need for acceptance and love kept me right in some mess that I could not get myself out of. From that day, things started to look up, at least that's what I thought, but people have a way of doing good for a moment to draw you back in, and boom, there goes the explosion again. I had endured so much trauma in the midst of that relationship that I became numb to the pain, and the fear of the unknown kept me bound. I'm not about to sit here and tell you I was a saint because a saint I was not. I eventually moved out of my grandmom's house and into my apartment, but no matter where I went, trouble was always present.

By that time, my mother was still going through a horrible marriage. It had gotten so bad that my younger siblings had to come live with me for a little while. I had no doubt that she could not have handled her own affairs because she was a strong-willed person. Her strength was unmatched. She had been through more adversity than the average person could have handled. My mom had three children by the time she was sixteen years old, and despite all the backlash she encountered, she still managed to graduate from high school with honors and a year early at that.

When I look at my mom now, I see a warrior. She was a strong, loving, caring, wise woman before her time full of wisdom.

My mom will give you the shirt off her back if needed. She loves people as well, and, just like me, she tries to see the good in everyone. How can you not love a woman who has the heart of God? Yeah, I was still hearing about God through the airways, but I was still unlearned in that area. So, I kept living the only way that I knew how to live, worldly. Fast forward to when my sisters finally came to live with me; they took on the same role as I did in my younger days. They helped me so much with my kids.

Yes, I somehow, along the way, found myself pregnant with another boy. At first, I was not overly excited about it because some horrible things transpired that resulted in me being pregnant, but I know God does not make any mistakes. So here I am with another bouncing baby boy whom I loved also dearly. Yes, I was becoming more knowledgeable about God, but I did not have a relationship with him. People can pretend to know him and confess out of their mouths that he is their Lord, but if their lifestyle has not changed, they are all doing lip service.

I am not ashamed to admit that I still did not know God and still had no intentions of pursuing a relationship with him. I still wanted to live my life without having any source of accountability to him. And like I said, even though my mom was going through her trials and tribulations, I too was going through them as well. The madness never stopped. It seemed like every man in my little city was afraid to say two words to me. They were afraid of my son's father. That man did so many horrible things that people began to call him little Scarface. Could you imagine having ties with someone that the world was afraid of?

I can only imagine what he had to do to be given a name like that. I was in constant fear for myself and my family. People in the streets could not have thought that I was at peace with whatever he was doing. After all none of what he acquired came into my home. It is no fun always looking over your shoulder wondering if someone is going to do something to you or your family because they could not find your kid's father. Oh yes, I received numerous phone calls, but I thank God because the friendships I made with these people from school caused them to rethink what they were planning to do. Even though you are unaware of God's presence protecting you, he is.

I had some praying family members, and because of the relationship they had with God, I know he heard their prayers. When my oldest son turned four, his father was sentenced to life in prison without parole. Whatever he was doing had come back to bite him in the end. It was heartbreaking to see his life go down in turmoil, but my greatest concern was that of my children. How was I going to tell them that their dad was given life in prison? It was a hard pill to swallow but a relief for me. I did not have to walk around in fear of the unknown anymore and despite all that I went through, I still had love for that man. Who would have thought that by the age of twenty-four years old, I would have endured all of that? But guess what? Life still had to go on.

Chapter 4

A New Leaf

After that season of my life was over, I began to work tirelessly to provide for my family. You wonder where I got that from. Yes, you are right, my hardworking mother. Even though back then, as a child, I did not understand the gravity of my mother's absent presence, I now realize that the same trait she possessed was instilled in me. Being a single mother is not for the weak, but having a great support system is God-given.

That does not mean that there were not times that I wanted to give up. I was drowning y'all, and on top of that, I found myself in and out of relationships, searching for love in all the wrong places. I did not know if I was coming or going. All I knew was that I had to be the best mother that I could be for my boys. They were full of life. So happy and unbothered. They did not have a care in the world. I made sure that no matter how tired I had become from working long hours at night I was present when they would awake in the mornings to see my face.

My heart melted every time I would see their little faces and their little smiles. Screams of "Mommy" would light my heart. They were the center of my joy. It was time for my boys and I to make a life transition, so we moved away from family, not much further than where we were at but guess what? My grandmother, who was in the nursing home, made that move with us. I was excited to be away from the city, but I was more excited that my grandmom was going to be living with us. I missed my grandma, and I am sure those people at that nursing home were glad to see her leave. She was a handful. So, I can imagine what she put them through.

My grandma was so funny. She would stir up some mess in the nursing home, call us up on the phone, and get us all rattled up and ready to fight, but when we got there, it was all a misunderstanding. All we could do was laugh about it and tell her she was a mess. But that was my grandma. If things did not go her way, you would hear about it. Long story short, Grandma got situated and began physical therapy in our home. She was wheelchair-bound, but that did not stop her from getting around.

One evening, while I was taking a nap before going to work, I awoke to my surprise to get ready for work, and Grandma was nowhere to be found. The boys were asleep in their rooms, but Grandma was gone. I called my mom on the phone, who at that time had recently moved around the corner from me. I said, "Mom, Grandma is gone with a trembling voice."

She said, "What do you mean your grandma is gone?" By that time, she had hung up the phone and run over to my apartment. She asked me, "When did you last see your grandma?"

I said, "Right before I took a nap." I had made sure everyone was well-fed, washed up, and ready for bed. After the boys were fast asleep, I helped my grandma into bed. I had gotten up, got ready for work, and, before heading out, went to check on everybody, but she was not there. It was nighttime, so where could she be? Mom and I went searching for her. Now, the apartment complex where I lived had upstairs and downstairs apartments. We did not have to look far because a couple of staircases down from my apartment, we found her wheelchair sitting.

Grandma had hoped in the car with some neighbors that she had never met before in her life and went to get her some cigarettes. I do not know about you, but I almost had a heart attack. She was always doing things of that nature. Physical therapy was doing her some good. Now let me remind you my grandmother had been through some things in her life that restricted her from being able to physically do a lot on her own, but that did not stop her. She was partially paralyzed on her left side. Which means it was dangerous for her to be doing a lot of the things she was doing.

To me, she was a dare-devil. Nothing was going to get in the way of what she wanted to accomplish. Now, that can be a good thing or a terrible thing, and in this case, it was bad. My grandmother was free to do whatever she wanted to do because if you told her she could not do it, she would do it anyway. She would trail around the neighborhood on her motorscooter, still enjoying life with a smile. But one day, I received a phone call from my mother letting me know that my grandma was over at their house.

My grandmother had somehow walked up the steps by herself to visit my mom and siblings, while she was unaware that grandma was on her way over there. Guess who had to come to help her down? That's right, me! By the time I reached my mom's apartment, my grandmother was sitting down in a chair at the top of the stairs, smoking a cigarette, eating donuts, and drinking coffee. If I were a volcano about to erupt, you could see the smoke ascending from my head. I was so angry with her, but she still had to be helped down the steps.

Thinking about those memories brings laughter and tears to my eyes. I told y'all she was something else. After ten long years of working in the nursing home, I decided to take a different route. Yes, I was a certified nurse's assistant and still am to this day. I loved my job. I loved taking care of elderly people, but it was beginning to take a toll on me. Not so much caring for them, but the fact that I felt like I was neglecting someone was hard for me to process. I would have anywhere from seventeen to twenty patients by myself. My coworkers and I occasionally helped each other out. But I was only one person, and if those lights were lit up, you knew someone needed your help.

The worst thing about it was if I was already busy helping someone else the other person had to suffer. If you have a heart and you genuinely care for people, that should bother you because it bothered me. So, I stepped away from working in a nursing facility and started working in Home Health Care. By this time, I had returned to the city again. I did not move into the city but more of the rural surrounding area, but I continued to work in this new field because the job was right up my alley. It was not a drastic change, but it sure did put my mind at peace. I was able to care for my patients and give them my undivided attention. I enjoyed caring for them and being able to spend time with them and their families. I met some great people who impacted my life while I was impacting theirs, too.

Shortly after turning over that new leaf. I began to pursue a new relationship with someone who had been a good friend of mine for over ten years. I was skeptical about being in a relationship with him because I did not want to ruin our friendship. But I will tell you this: when you cross those boundaries, you had better be ready to deal with all the skeletons you knew not of. If I had known just a snippet of what I was going to encounter, I would have run like a terrified dog with its tail curled under him.

Within the first three months, I knew that this relationship was going to be a rollercoaster ride. I ended up pregnant and carrying a beautiful baby girl. I am not going to say I was shocked because I was doing grown-up stuff, I had no business doing until I was married. Our relationship continued to progress, and I continued to do what I loved to do best, which was take care of those that were in need. I was committed to helping my patients with their continued journey of life so that they would not feel like they were a burden to their families.

I enjoyed taking them on outings, doctor's appointments, and things of that nature, even though it was forbidden to do so. It broke my heart to see how some of them viewed life in the state that they were in. No one should have to feel like their life is over because they did not have the mobility they once had in their younger days. So, breaking a little rule did not matter to me. To see the smiles on their faces and youthfulness glow back restored warmed my heart. But the pregnancy had begun to take a toll on me once again. I could not keep anything down, but still, I pressed my way through. Even some of my clients felt bad for me.

They started sending me home after I finished taking care of their main needs. Also, the stress of a verbally abusive relationship had me walking on eggshells. When most of the pregnancy sickness subsided, my daughter's father came to live with me. Why did I make that hasty decision? There were times when he had to drop me off at work, and we argued because the client's family members were visiting their homes. That man thought every man and their momma wanted to be in a relationship with me. I thought that I was insecure, but that was another level of insecurity for me.

Those arguments lasted the entire time I was in a relationship with him. I just knew that this was a relationship that was going to be hard to get out of. During this time, I still did not have a relationship with God, but it did not stop me from praying to him. I just knew that if he could bring me out of this relationship, I would not have to suffer through the heartache and pain that I went through with my boy's father. I heard many testimonies of what God did in the lives of people I was connected to. Who was I to doubt what he did for them? Unaware that God was increasing my faith in Him I just knew if he did it for them, he could do it for me.

I know now that we overcome trials by the blood of Jesus and one another's testimonies. God sometimes will allow you to go through fiery trials until you surrender your will for his. I did not know what that meant at the time, but all I wanted to do was be free. I knew I had gotten myself into a world of trouble, but I could not give in to the pressure that was trying to overtake me. My daughter's father and I split up for a little while. When it was time for me to give birth to my daughter, like a repeated cycle, I gave back into all the empty promises and sweet nothings.

I ended up losing my apartment and moving back in with my mom. The strain of trying to work and maintain bills on my own while having to take maternity leave unexpectedly was not enough finances to keep me afloat. Thank God I had a caring mother that supported me no matter what. I know some of you are wondering why I keep talking about God like I had a relationship with him. But that is how some claim to know him but only know of him.

Two days before Christmas in the year of twenty-thirteen, my little bundle of joy was born. Of course, her father was in the room to help welcome our beautiful baby girl. I was so excited because before I had gotten pregnant with her, I had developed a seven-centimeter cyst on my left ovary, and doctors told me that because of the magnitude of the cyst, I had to have one of my ovaries removed. I was devastated. They also expressed that it would but more difficult for me to conceive. Those words crushed my spirit because I wanted a baby girl so bad. But guess what happened?

A week later, I went through surgery to remove the cyst, and it had disappeared. Look at God. My mom and I, and even her boss at that time, had prayed that God would move on my behalf, and he did just that. Another encounter and miracle that God performed. The doctors were puzzled. You could not tell me what God could not do. I was talking like a Holy Ghost-filled Christian at that moment. Praising him and thanking him for what he had done for me. On Christmas day, I was able to leave the hospital to go home and enjoy all my family. I was not planning to have any more children, so before leaving, I made the decision to get my tubes tied.

Chapter 5
No More

After returning home, I continued to go through more turmoil. I was tired of trying to save someone from living a life of destruction when it was not possible for me to do it in the first place. All the back-and-forth breaking up just to make up shenanigans was not worth it. I needed peace of mind to care for my kids. I decided to part ways with him even though I was terrified of the outcome. I had already seen my share of what an unstable mind could do, but still, I packed all his belongings and proceeded to take him to one of his relatives' houses.

While we were driving en route, he snatched the steering wheel, which almost caused us to drive into a ditch. I pulled over to a gas station, grabbed my kids out of the backseat, and ran into the store. The manager called the police for me, and they took him to his uncle's house. I did not want him to go to jail. I just wanted him as far away as possible from me. Even though I went through all of that I still had love for this man. That incident was enough for me to call it quits. At least, that is how I felt at that moment. You could be so blinded by the perception of love that you dismiss harm when it presents itself right in front of you.

That was me, still broken and willing to give love another try despite all the bad relationships I went through. This time, we separated for a long time. I figured time apart would do us some justice, but, in the meantime, I went back to work. I saved up enough money to live on my own again and my other grandma, my dad's mom, had come to live with me. I loved my grandma, but this woman was a handful, too. She lived with me for about two years, and in the process of living with me, I found myself fighting demons within myself.

My grandmother was a God-fearing woman also. What have I gotten myself into? Our sleeping schedules were opposite of one another, and she stayed up all night playing her gospel music. I would wake up and go into the living room to ask her if she could turn the music down, and unbeknownst to me, she had company over in the early hours of the morning. Oh, they were having a blast singing their gospel music and just talking about the Lord.

We had our difficulties, but my grandma was the type who would make you sit down and hear what she had to say about the Lord. Now, that is what you call a woman on a mission for God, but I still did not want to hear about it because my mind was not focused on the Lord. We would often bump heads, but she instilled a lot of knowledge about God in me. I still did not realize that God was trying to get my attention then. You know the knowledge of Christ is foolishness to those who are perishing, and it was sad to say I was still perishing in the world.

My grandmother would sit in the house, write gospel music, create a new sound on her keyboard, and sing her songs to God. My children were so infatuated with her. They gravitated so easily to her spirit while she lived with us. Sometimes, she would get all dressed up like she was going to catch a man and head off to church. Later, I found out that the man she was looking for was Jesus and she did find him. My grandma once told me that she had a disease that was incurable, but after Jesus had gotten a hold of her, he healed her body completely. I could not deny the power of God working in her life because I had experienced some things back then that I give credit to God for now.

My mom's mother had moved in with her and when she needed a break, she would send my grandma over for a while to spend time with us all. What do you call two Holy Ghost-filled women when they get together? A forest fire because when they yoked up together, every demon on the block had to flee, including me. They were already too much to handle separately. Now I had both grandmas in one house having church. On the other hand, my children loved being in the company of both of their great-grandmas. That was a blessing to see. They had a great friendship. After a while, Grandma wanted to move back to her old neighborhood.

We were sad to see her go but now I was able to get back in the groove of things. My daughter's father was going through hardships, and I decided to let him move into the house to get himself together. Besides, it was nice because my daughter was able to see her father every day and create a bond with him. He was also attentive to my boys as well. He had his own room; we were able to co-parent without interfering in each other's affairs.

That lasted for a while until his efforts to change and wanting his family back were noticeable. When I tell you, the devil can dress up distractions so well just to get you to fall right back into his traps. We gave it another try. Things were going well as he started creating a bond with all the children. Increasingly, I became curious about God, and on occasions, as a family, we started visiting a church recommended by my mother. It did not take long for the arguments to resurface, and then pop goes the weasel. I had to make a conscious choice to just let bygones be bygones and go our separate ways. So, towards the middle of twenty-sixteen, we parted ways, and I never looked back.

That did not stop my daughter's father from making threats towards me and himself, but when you are done, you are done. When my daughter's father finally left, she would tell me stories about monsters that she always seen in her room at nighttime. I was already a little leery of some of the things my daughter would say because one time before her father came to live with us, I had picked her up from daycare, and she asked me why her dad was arguing and fighting with the police officers in his hometown because now he ended up in jail.

I dismissed what she said and tried to call him so that she could speak with him, but I did not get an answer. I began to search the website for inmates who were booked within twenty-four hours, and when I typed in his name, he was right there, incarcerated for exactly what she had told me. To make matters worse, around the same time I picked her up from daycare, he was booked into jail at that time. I was flabbergasted and scared. I had heard about prophets in the Bible but that threw me for a loop. I called up my cousin and asked her to pray over at my house.

I was a little knowledgeable about demons and unclean spirits, but I was not equipped to handle that. I had not given my life to Christ yet. Work started to become remarkably interesting as I accepted a new client who happened to be a pastor. I was still attending church here and there, and of course, my new client and his wife were imparting the Word of God inside of me. I thought to myself, "God, you really do have a sense of humor." Out of all the people in the world I could have been connected to, it had to be a pastor.

Sometimes, my client would have a Bible Study session going on at his house when I arrived, I had no choice but to join right in, and I was not even angry about it. Those two became the first spiritual parents I had. They were both loving and caring people who would do anything for someone in need. I became a part of their family, and they became a part of mine.

Meanwhile, the feelings of loneliness continued to pursue me, and there I was again in another relationship. This relationship was different than those that I previously was in. This man was kind, not verbally, physically, or mentally abusive. He had some great qualities that caught my attention. He was the first man that I had dealings with that was non-confrontational. Things were going well. We were getting acquainted with one another. He wined and dined me, and that was something I was not used to.

I had been self-sufficient for so long that I did not know how to receive help if it hit me in the face. I was used to people claiming to do things from their hearts but ending up throwing it back in my face. That left a bad taste in my mouth, so I did not accept anything from anyone outside of my family. It was hard for me to ask them for help as well. But I am often reminded that sometimes, to receive something you first must open your mouth and ask for it. God surely had to work on me in that area. In trying to pursue this relationship, I found myself drifting away from God altogether.

I wanted this relationship to work, but about six months in, I distinctly heard God tell me he was not the one for me. Those words were ignored because I thought I had finally found someone who appreciated me and treated me right. There was only one problem with him in my eyesight and that was he was not a believer in Christ. I was not committed to Christ yet either, but I knew he was calling me into a relationship with him. I would always sit and talk with my cousin and tell her how I wanted a man who would treat me right and have a heart after God.

I even told her that I wanted to marry a pastor one day. But this man was not a bad person. He was family-oriented, which meant the world to me because I had children, and if anyone would not accept my children then you could not have thought any type of relationship with me would have existed. My children were blessings from God, and I would not ever want them to experience the things I had to grow up with. Well, this man worked as a contractor, and wherever his employer received a contract for work, he had to go. I was okay with that at first because he was not gone for extended periods of time, but when he started being away for months at a time, I began to get frustrated.

The tables had finally turned. Here I was, pouring my heart out and not receiving anything in return but a bunch of excuses. This went on for the remainder of the year until, finally, I had to call it quits. I mean, God had already tried to warm me, but silly ole me I was still trying to fill a void inside of me. At the beginning of twenty-seventeen, I was single again. This time, I was so damaged that thoughts of suicide began to creep into my mind. I started questioning God, why me? Why can't I find anyone to love me? What is wrong with me? Do I not deserve a happy life? Why is everything always going wrong for me? Why did you create me? If I took my life, would anyone even care?

Yes, me. I was drowning in silence, battling all kinds of things. And in that moment, the only thing that kept me afloat was knowing that if I succumbed to these negative thoughts, my children would be the ones suffering. Darkness was slowly consuming me, but I had to keep trying to press my way through.

Chapter 6

Finding God

Back then, I was a social media junkie. I had a filthy mouth. I posted all kinds of nasty things, from sexually explicit memes and enticing pictures of myself, even to the point where I would join in with others' corrupt conversations. One day, I was strolling down my timeline, and I came across a flyer that was surfacing about a revival. By this time, I had stopped attending church altogether. What was the purpose of going if nothing was changing in my life? So, I called up one of my sisters to see if she wanted to attend this revival with me. She could not make it. I was hesitant to go, but I went on my own. \

When God is calling you into a certain place, sometimes you must take that walk alone so that he can have your undivided attention. I was scared because when I attended the revival, I saw people being called up for prayer, and as soon as the Man of God laid his hands on them, they were dropping like flies trapped in a closed-up car on a scorching summer day. My mind told me it was time to exit the building, but my heart would not let me leave. I saw people being healed, delivered, saved, and set free by God's power working through his people. It was like nothing I had ever seen before. I mean, I heard about these types of signs, miracles, and wonders, but to see them firsthand was amazing.

My belief in God went straight through the roof. As I was sitting there enjoying the word and praising God, I saw the guest preacher, who was also a prophet of the Lord, continuously glancing at me. I said to myself, "Why does this man keep looking at me," I began to put my head down so that I could not see him looking at me, and then the unthinkable thing happened. He points at me and calls me to the front of the church. I turned my head and looked behind me as if he were talking to someone else.

He said, "I am talking to you, a woman of God while pointing his finger at me. I was afraid. I did not want to go in front of the whole church let alone be one of those people who were falling like flies. I might have talked about all that foolishness on social media, but in person, I was very timid. I did not like to be in large crowds anymore, and I did not want to be noticed. I had dug a ditch for myself and closed off the world. So, he proceeded to say to me, "I know that you are afraid, but God wants to speak to you." I got up and went to the front of the church, and this man began to tell me about things I had been through in the past and what I was going through then. How could this be that a stranger knew personal details about me?

I began to weep, and at that very moment, I knew that there was a God. In February year two thousand-eighteen I gave my life to Christ and never looked back. Yes, I ended up slain in the spirit laid out on the floor just like the rest of them, but when I got up off the floor, I felt refreshed. I had come from among the world's ways of living entirely. I was excited to start my new journey with Christ. I found myself with my head indulged in the Bible every chance I got.

The relationship I was building with him was unexplainable. If you had asked my kids at that time what my hobbies were, their answer would have been going to church and reading the Bible. Shortly after receiving salvation from the Lord, I joined the church I was visiting. I not only had a Pastor and First Lady that poured into me, but I also had a church family that made me feel welcome. More knowledge, more power, and the Holy Ghost went to work in my life. I began to see myself in a different light.

God had opened my eyes to a whole new world and way of living. He showed me things about myself that I never knew. He not only showed me who he was and who I was in him, he showed me who I belonged to, which was him. He also taught me what it meant to surrender to his will. I was all in. I had no intentions of going back into the world because, in that brief period of getting to know him, I had already fallen in love with him. It was the best feeling I had ever felt before. I started attending church services regularly, getting acquainted with my new family, and growing in the knowledge of Christ.

Of course, my children were right by my side. I wanted to be a godly example for them instead of what they were used to in the past. The Bible tells us to train our children in the way they should go, and when they are old, they will not depart from it. So, that is what I started doing. Every time I was there, they were there. It did not matter if they wanted to go or not, but to my surprise, they enjoyed going. It was especially important to me that my kids were getting fed as well. The church's children's ministry was impactable. Those who were over the ministry would teach them about God in a way that ministered to children in their generation. It was unorthodox, spirit-led, and fun to witness. My children had fun, and so did I.

We would help gather up kids from around the community no matter what church they attended because, in God's eyes, we were all one body. So, we brought them so that they could experience God for themselves. This also gave parents a little free time to themselves. It was great for the community because children had a place that they could be free in God and not get sucked into the street life. Sometimes, they would bring in other young believers to pour into the children. I remember sitting in on a session, and the kids were asking questions about certain situations they were dealing with. One young girl asked a question about death, you know, life after death, and the whole session shifted down a different path. It just made me take a moment to pause and see that adults are not the only ones dealing with life's issues.

These kids were experiencing the same things that we sometimes go through. It was heartbreaking to hear but they received a great teaching and understanding of what is to come. They prayed together, laughed together, sang together, and danced together. It was a joyous moment to see children be free and encouraged along the way. That is what you call doing work for God. We must reach people from different walks of life, including children. They are the next generation of believers.

A few months into communing with God I could see that he was changing the way I talked. I told y'all I had a filthy mouth. I cursed like a sailor. But he took that filthiness away from me completely. I was shocked but praised him the more. I was happy to be a part of a body of believers who made a difference in the community. There was a ministry called Feed the City that warmed my heart. We would prepare lunch bags for those who were homeless or in need, head out into the community, and pray with those who received the lunch bags. That was one of the highlights of my day. Even though I was a little timid that did not stop me from agreeing with what was prayed over them.

The Bible speaks about praying together on one accord and God answering prayers. I loved to see God move in people's lives. It not only increased my faith but gave me hope. Another ministry within the church I looked forward to was called Balling for Jesus. I had never seen anything like it before. It was a huge community shebang. This outreach ministry prepared children with the necessities they needed to begin the new school year.

They received brand new backpacks, composition notebooks, looseleaf paper, pencils, pens, two pocket folders, binders, crayons, colored pencils, glue sticks, sizers, you name it. Whatever you could think of, it was there. It even provided families with basic hygiene necessities as well. It was a fun atmosphere for everyone to attend. There was music, free food, games, and prizes that people could win.

Everyone had a blast. Not only did other church ministries from around the community volunteer to help serve and make this outreach a success, but it was also a great way to reach people and show the love of Christ. Sponsors from all over started pouring into this outreach until it began to spread throughout other counties. The Lord was surely in the midst of this ministry. The biggest highlight of the day was a basketball tournament that was held for children to participate in. Not only was the church involved, but the county's police department showed up with their support as well.

It was like something you would see in a movie that caught the attention of the world. Kingdom work was being done right before my eyes, and I was in the midst of it all. I am not going to sit up here and say that I was comfortable in the beginning because I had never seen that many people come together as a whole in my life without any violence being present.

In that very moment I got a glimpse of how heaven would be with everyone getting alone while being in the presence of God. When you decide to give your life to Christ, all kinds of attacks from the enemy begin to come at you, and the church has a ministry called (ASAP) Always Stop And Pray. If you were going through a situation and you needed someone to pray with you and for you, you could stop by the church and get what you needed.

That was a blessing because when I tell you the enemy came in like a flood of water that destroyed a city, I mean just that. His power could not defeat the power of God. God's power was unmatched. I began attending their Women's Ministry so that I could be with women who would cover me in prayer. It was awesome. At first, I was not too excited about gathering with a lot of women because I had my share of backstabbers in my younger days, but this was different.

These women cared about your walk with Christ. It was not until there that God truly began to deal with my heart and bring up things from my past that I had suppressed. Those memories were painful. I did not want to relive them again, but who was I to tell God no. Being born again is about being transformed into the image of Christ so there I found myself allowing God to open up wounds that were only covered with a bandage. People were able to talk about things they encountered throughout life with the hopes of things being confidential. I was stubborn. I did not want these people all up in my business, so I stayed quiet for a while, listened, and learned to be honest with God so that my healing would come forth.

Chapter 7
Healing

When it comes to being healed, you must first acknowledge that you need help, surrender to God, and allow him to be all up in your space. We must make room for him. We are the temples that house the Holy Spirit, and we cannot allow our temples to become tainted. God had a magnificent work to do inside of me, and it started with the hate I had for my son's father. That may not have been the first broken pieces within me but the fact that I was harboring hate for this man prompted God to quickly intervene.

The Bible tells us that if we hate our brother or sister, we are considered murderers, and there is no way we could have Christ living inside of us with that type of heart. I did not realize that because of the hardships I went through with him in the past could have caused me to not be able to enter God's kingdom. I now know that God is love and that we are to pray for those who mistreat us, but back then, that was nowhere near my mind nor in my heart. How could I forgive someone who repeatedly broke my heart, abused me, and took me for granted?

God had to show me that when I was not in his will and lived among the world, I was doing that very same thing to him. I was repeatedly breaking his heart and taking his love, his grace, and his mercy for granted. He had to show me that as many times as I took my son's father back, he did the same for me.

Even though I hurt him daily, he continued to give me a chance after chance after chance, and even though I put up with my son's father's mess, he put up with mine. He had to show me that even though I chose their dad to be my God over him, he never gave up loving me, he never pushed me aside, he never stopped trying to get my attention, he continued to have patience with me, he continued to love me past my flaws, he continued to protect me and shield me, he continued to have compassion on me, and he continued to even bless me in the midst of it all, and for that, I am forever grateful unto him. He never left me hanging. He always provided for me and gave me a way to escape, even though I took a different route. He always listened to me, heard my cries, and answered my prayers.

Not one time did he ever abandon me, and most importantly, he forgave me repeatedly and never brought up my sinful past. I was not aware of his beautiful presence in the midst of all that turmoil. I had no choice but to swallow my pride and allow God to massage my heart because I did not want to be someone who saw hell as their home. God told me that if I did not forgive my son's father, he was not going to forgive me. So, I had to straighten up quickly. It was not easy to forgive him, but I wanted Christ more than anything this world had to offer. I allowed him to take that small portion of unforgiveness out of my heart and teach me how to forgive myself and not hold on to the hurt.

God was trying to give me a new heart, and to be free, I had to surrender and receive my healing. God is constantly trying to teach us that love covers a multitude of sins and that we are not supposed to hate people but rather the sin inside of them. Once I forgave their father, God allowed their father to send me a letter from prison apologizing for everything that he had done and put me through. Look at God. I was relieved and a weight was lifted off me. When you are truly healed, you no longer feel any type of ill will feelings towards a person.

I knew that God had healed me because the mention of his name did not get a negative reaction or response out of me. Those suppressed feelings were gone, and that was the beginning of my healing process. For every trail and storm I endured God had to peel back old layers of my past to be able to mold me into who he created me to be. There was purpose in my pain, and growth in him had to come forth. I now embrace the storms of life because I know that in them all, God is present and trying to condition me for what is to come, purge me of things within myself that he is not pleased with, and teach me how to become a matured Christian whose light can shine for him.

As I continued to grow in the knowledge of Christ, it became clear to me why I could not remain upset with people for an extended period. Back then, people could do things to hurt me, and I would easily forgive them even though I did not want to. I wanted to be mad. I wanted to fall out with people and dismiss them from my life but the love for people that was already inside of me would not let me be that horrible person. God's attributes were always there because his breath was inside of me from the beginning.

Even though I was molested as a child however, in my adult years as a Christian woman, I brought that same person to church with me so that he could receive what he needed from Christ. No matter what you go through in life, you must understand that everyone deserves a second chance. This is the very reason that Christ died for our sins so that we could be reconciled back to God. There is no big sin or little sin. It is all sin in God's eyes, and whether we agree or disagree with what someone has done, God is their judge. We will all have to account for whatever it is that we did or said in our lifetime. That man needed God just as bad as I did so who was I to stop Him from having an encounter with Christ? I received my healing and wanted him to receive his as well. With healing comes deliverance, and The Potter was making me brand new, and I loved it.

Chapter 8
Caught off Guard

I know that God tells us to be alert and watchful, but this next chapter of my life caught me off guard. As I was minding my own business in the Lord like Ruth did in the Bible, out of nowhere, I got an instant message on social media from a Man of God who was also a prophet of the Lord that I did not know. This man had begun to speak into my life and tell me personal details about myself that he could only have known because of God. God will tell all your business (smiling while shaking my head), but how else will someone who is not a believer in him know that he is real? I knew it was God, but some of the things this man told me caught me off guard.

After telling me something of significance he proceeded to tell me about a man that would be coming into my life in the year of two-thousand and nineteen. He did not specifically tell me what for, but all I knew was he was coming. Just for a split second, I rebuked that part of the prophecy because I was not looking for a man. When it said in the Bible that an unmarried person can focus on pleasing God, I took that to heart. I did not want anything or anyone to come between my relationship with Christ, but God had other plans for me. Long story short, two months after I received that prophecy, there appeared out of nowhere a man who was interested in me. I began to look at God with a side eye because he knew that I had told him that I was not ready. God is humorous at times.

You know, sometimes we can get bossy and try to tell God what we are not going to do, only for him to show us who is in charge. I told God that I was not about to be in a relationship with someone I met on social media. I tried that avenue in the past, and it did not work out well, so I was not too fond of entertaining it again. This man messaged me a few days after I liked his picture. Yes, I was just strolling through social media and liked his picture first. He was very handsome and well-dressed, so I hit the thumbs up and kept it moving.

I was not expecting anything in return, but a few days later, when I opened my messaging app, there was a message waiting for me. At that time, I did not have the messenger app downloaded for the very purpose that I spoke about. I did not need any distractions coming my way. I looked at the messages and did not respond. To be honest, I did not even know how to respond to him because I had only been single and in Christ for a year and a half. I knew I could not respond to him in the way the world responded to people, so I had to call up my cousin, who also was a Woman of God, for some pointers.

To my surprise she knew this man and proceeded to tell me

that he was a nice Man of God. I listened to all the good things she had to say about him including a little personal background on him, and I let it marinate in my head for a while. The next day, I responded to his messages. Prior to that, my regular routines consisted of going to work, going to school, taking care of my children, going to church, and being true to my Lord and Savior Jesus Christ.

I had no time for games because God had already brought me a long way from where I was then. I was doing simply fine getting to know myself. I did not allow myself to engage in foolery. God had healed me completely before he decided to bring someone into my life, and I had to accept that he knew what was best for me. Over the course of two months of getting to know this man, God had already told me that he was my husband. I never told him. I just waited patiently for God to reveal it to him, and guess what, y'all? It took two long years. Even though it took two years, we were still getting acquainted with each other. We communicated on the phone for a while before I decided to go on a date with him.

We would talk for hours on the phone and refuse to hang up with one another. We acted like teenagers when we could talk on the phone with our crush and would run out of things to say and listen to each other breathe. That was us enjoying each other's conversation and company. We talked together, laughed together, prayed together, and spent a lot of time together. For a while, this man would not come into the front gate of my fence. He had that much respect for me, and I found that very intriguing. That was something I was not used to. So, I went to God in prayer.

You know, sometimes, when things seem too good to be true, you immediately go to the father for answers. I had to ask my father who was this man he sent into my life and what was he hiding that I could not see. Be careful what you pray for because God will show you. The very next day, God showed me something concerning this man, but it only revealed to me that no one is perfect. Only Christ is. It did not scare me away because God told me I was going to be a part of his healing process, so I trusted him and proceeded with anticipation.

Our conversations started to get deeper beyond the surface of getting to know someone in that early stage. I felt like I had known this man for years until suddenly, things began to shift between us, and boom, he was gone like a genie in a movie who had fulfilled his three wishes unto his master. I had become vulnerable with this man and let him into my heart because I did wear it on my sleeve, but when things took a turn for what seemed the worse for me, I leaned on God for what I needed at that moment, his love, his comfort, his reassurance, and peace. I thought I was doing a decent job at guarding my heart, but in that brief time, the enemy had taken me back to a familiar place that I did not want to be.

Thank God that Christ was on my side because healing became easy in that season of my life. Sometimes, God will give you a glimpse of the promises he has for you, but if it is not in his timing for it to be manifested and you disobey him in the process, he will prolong what he has for you until the timing is right. God had more pruning to do inside of me, and more growth in him needed to be revealed. So once again, I dived back into his word and kept my focus on him and him only.

After a while I realized that before communicating with this man, I had seen him in passing at a couple of church functions around the community. I had never taken a second look at him because, at that time, I was not interested in the idea of being with anyone. It is funny how God can allow you to be in the midst of someone's presence and not even know they exist. Besides, God was already grooming him for the attacks that he would face. What he was going through was enough for someone who did not know Christ to give up altogether.

There were multiple deaths in his family back-to-back. He had recently lost the mother of his youngest daughter, who he was married to, and then there was the death of his brother all in the same month. In the midst of all he was going through, he remarried and divorced quickly. So, that nine-month break was necessary. Healing needed to take place, and that is what happened. On the day of my birthday, June 2, two-thousand and twenty, God allowed us to cross paths again.

I still considered this man a friend because even though things did not align for us then he was still a brother in Christ that was dear to my heart. My cousin and I headed to the grocery store to pick up a couple of items, and there stood a familiar face across the parking lot. He had his youngest daughter with him who I had already fallen in love with, and she spots me and sprints across the parking lot to greet me. The look on his face told me that he was not expecting his daughter to react like that, let alone run into my arms as if it had been years since she had seen me. She missed me, and I missed her, and he had no choice but to come and greet my cousin and me. We said our hellos and goodbyes and continued with our day. I found out that when God has a plan in motion, there is nothing you can do to stop it. Shortly after my cousin and I arrived back home, my brother in Christ (because that is what I called him) showed up at my house and we picked right up from where we left off. It was crazy. It seemed as if nothing had happened, but there we were, continuing what God had started.

In the process of rekindling our friendship my grandmother had taken sick. My mom called me from the hospital and said that things were not going well with my grandmother and that the whole family was gathering to see her before things took a turn for the worse. So, I hurried to the hospital with my children and waited in the lobby along with other family members who were there for my chance to see her.

As I waited, I received a phone call from my brother in Christ. He wanted to come show his support and be by my side through that challenging time, but I insisted that he did not have to come. He ended up coming anyway, and as soon as he walked through the door, all eyes were on him. I was so embarrassed because I had never brought a man around my family unless I was serious about them, and on top of that, we were not even dating. I could tell by the looks on their faces that they had already concluded that he was more than just a friend. I knew that when it came time for me to see my grandmother, the family would discuss what they had just witnessed. And boy, there was a mouthful said. One of my sisters had already started calling him bae, but I paid her no mind at all. He accompanied me to see her, and before we could get into the room, you could see the big stares and hear the whispers of other family members asking who he was. I paid them no mind, too, and walked in to see my grandmother.

It was a sad day for us all, but we knew that if God took her home that day, it was her time to go. While in her room, those still in there circled around and held hands as he led us in prayer. I was shocked that that man took time out of his busy schedule to be by my side and pray for us and with us. That made me look at him in a different light. I mean, I knew he was a pastor and all but who would have thought that God was answering another one of my prayers?

That was not the day that God called my grandmother home, praise God, but her time was near, and when she finally left us, it was a joyous moment for me because she was not suffering any longer. I knew where she was going and that was to see our father in heaven, whom she had longed for some time.

Around this time, I quit working in the home health field and took a job with the school board. I was working as a clinic assistant, and I am still there currently. The love that I had for people and their well-being will never cease. It did not matter what career I invested in caring for people was in my nature. That was a time when Covid had begun to run rampant throughout the world, and schools worldwide were closed. There I was trying to adjust to being a mother who wore many other hats and a teacher.

That was a challenging season to go through but my faith in God remained as we were still allowed to fellowship in church. Our church was one of the few that did not close due to Covid. That was a blessing because I was still able to go to rehearsal and get my praise. I was the praise and worship leader at our church, and I currently hold that position. Ever since I was a little girl, I wanted to be a part of a choir. And look how God made that possible. It does not matter how young or old you are. When you have a calling from God on your life, and you accept the call things that you may have desired at an early age can be manifested right before your eyes.

He said that he will give you the desires of your heart if you delight in him, and that is just what I did. I loved fellowshipping with the team. It was a bit of a struggle in the beginning, but that was nothing, prayer, humility, and communication could not cure. I complained in the beginning as well, but I had to learn to take everything to God and be the leader that he called me to be. I was not comfortable with correcting someone about things that could help them grow in their gifts from God because I did not want to offend anyone, but when it came to God's work, everything had to be spirit-led first, done with order, excellence, and in love.

We are supposed to sharpen each other and encourage one another along the way. Chastisement and growth in God had to first reach me before I could effectively teach others. I thought I was not equipped to lead the praise and worship team because I was unlearned, but I now know that God qualifies those that he calls, and before he formed me in my mother's womb, he had already set me apart to do great works for him. Nobody has it all together, and we are constantly learning and perfecting what God has entrusted us with. Worship was not just praising God. It was a lifestyle but when I got a chance to pour out my everything to him, I got the breakthrough that I needed.

Singing to him and thanking him for who he was and what he had done in my life was what I lived for. His presence in my life meant everything to me. I could never have stopped praising God because he had been too good to me. There was a difference between being gifted and anointed. Everybody could sing, but the anointing was needed for yokes to be broken off people's lives. People came to church bound, fighting with demons and feeling trapped inside, but when God's power reached them, they were freed from whatever it was that they were going through. We know that Satan comes to sift us like wheat, but the power of God eliminates everything that he tries to use to destroy us. In Christ, we are conquerors, and there is nothing that Satan can do about it.

Chapter 9
Tried and True

The more I grew closer to God, the greater the attacks became. The magnitude of this test almost made me lose my mind, but God. When I tell you Satan tried to not only take me out, but he also tried to take my son out as well, and I mean just that. All hell was beginning to break loose in my house, and people watched and talked about what they could only see from the outside. I tried to shelter my children from hanging in the streets and being one of those people that someone in authority could have labeled as being a thug.

I did not want them to fall accustomed to the ways of the world. In our society today, black adults are not the only ones murdered by law enforcement. Young children were being targeted, too. This is not to say that it was only black people that were being murdered. Other races were also suffering. I would be considered a liar if I said that I was not afraid of what the outcome could have been, but it was something I did not want to happen to my children, let alone anyone else's.

It seemed like the more I tried to shelter my children from the world, the more my oldest son wanted to be a part of it. He had gotten a taste of it and that was enough for him to want to do whatever he wanted to do without consulting me first. I mean, he was only a teenager at that time, but as his mother, a now woman of God, I was not about to let him go down a pathway of destruction. So, to God, I went in prayer. I had been through enough battles to know that there were many weapons I could have chosen to use against Satan, but prayer and fasting were the weapons I chose.

I prayed, and I fasted for what seemed like forever, but God showed up and turned that situation around for his good and ours. For those of you who may be dealing with rebellious children, my advice to you would be to give them back to God and never stop praying for them. God wanted to see who my faith was when he allowed the enemy to infiltrate my camp. You know before the enemy can touch you, he must get permission from God first. Just like Job in the Bible, he was given access to test me. I could feel the flames of the fire that was heating up right in my own home.

My son had chosen to hang out with the wrong crowd of people and get involved with a girl that was not the best choice for him from what I could see. I am not saying that my son was a saint, but he knew what was expected of him, and he knew where a lifestyle of hell could lead him, but like I said, it was his choice. Nobody can make you do anything you do not want to do unless you are in a situation that you have no control over. It is just like Jesus offering salvation to you. It is your choice to receive it. If you do not receive it, then you know what the outcome is, fire and brimstone and gnashing of teeth.

The Bible clearly tells us to be careful who we hang around because bad company can corrupt good character, and he knew better. Yet he insisted on testing me. That was a test and a testimony for both of us. Halfway through his first two years of high school, he had begun to skip school, smoke marijuana, party, and not come home, disrespect me verbally, and God knows what when he was not in my presence. I even ended up getting a few phone calls from law enforcement because of his reckless driving in the neighborhood. All of that resulted in him dropping out of school in the last semester of tenth grade.

Boy, was I angry? I was at wit's end with him. I reached out to a few of my family members and my pastor to try and talk with him but all that did was push him further away. In his mind, he was a grown man, so I decided to treat him as such. If he did not want to respect me and abide by my rules, then he could do what adults do, provide for themselves. After seeking godly counsel from those within my circle, I had begun to establish boundaries in my house that I could control, and whatever was out of my reach that I could not control, I did not worry about it.

Now, remember that I was still trying to be a godly example in that chaos raising my two younger children. Some of the boundaries that were put in place were all my entry doors and windows being locked at a specific time, and if he did not make it home in time, he needed to find somewhere else to lay his head. He had already lost the keys to the house so there was no reason to get a new set for him.

Another boundary was not giving him access to drive my car. You know, as parents, we oftentimes allow our children to have access to certain things as we sacrifice necessities to make ends meet, but it was a privilege to be able to drive my car, and once the disrespect started, that was revoked. If he had wanted to go somewhere and it was not a necessity, then he needed to find a way on his own to get there. When I left to go to work, and he made a choice to skip school everything was locked up until I returned home from work. Now, while at home, he had access to every necessity that he needed in our house, including food, but if he wanted anything extra that required money, he could not get it from me.

I know to some it may seem harsh, but we as parents should not allow our children to be disrespectful in any way, shape, form, or fashion to us, let alone other adults, and think that it is okay. We are parents first and God has entrusted us with our children to teach them how to be able to distinguish right from wrong and make godly moral decisions.

It is a requirement from God to be holy as he is, and that is exactly what I was trying to instruct my children to do. Christ-like character is more valuable than the things of this world and that is a way for people to differentiate you from the world. They know who you belong to by the fruit that you bear. This battle was too much for me to fight on my own, so I gave it and him to God. After all, God had already known exactly what he was dealing with because he was the one who created him.

Our battles do not belong to us. They belong to God. So why do we as people keep holding on to battles and trying to fight them in our own strength when God said his strength is made perfect in our weakness. Nope! Not me! I gave it to God for the sake of my sanity. Sometimes, we as parents forget that Satan is not only after us, but he is after our children, too. They have callings on their lives from God and he sometimes must take them through situations to get their attention as well. They are going to go through hardships in their lives where God must intervene and show himself to them. They must receive salvation from God for themselves and have their own personal relationship with Christ, too.

Even though things were going horribly wrong at that time, I continued to praise God through it all because trusting him and drawing near to him was the only way I was going to pass that test. It was hard, but it was he who I needed most of all to have victory, and the victory was received. We were not out of the woodwork, yet my son ended up running away from home, and that broke my heart.

I was distraught. Feelings of doubt and fear had begun to creep into my mind.

The enemy kept whispering in my ear that I was a horrible parent, but there was nothing that I could do but continue to cover him in prayer. Eventually, God had brought him back home, but in all of that there was a lesson from God that I needed to learn. He told me that just as my son had become rebellious and ran off into the world, I, too, needed to remember that I was once in that same place. He said that there were many times that I did things that went against his instruction as a father, yet he welcomed me back with open arms as the prodigal son did in the Bible.

He told me that I needed to reconcile with my son and not hold things against him because he was not perfect, nor was I. He told me to forgive him like he did me and never to bring up that situation as a condemning moment to him. He told me to continue to show him that I love him and that we all make mistakes, but it is what we do with those mistakes in the end that truly matters. Are we going to learn from them or allow them to keep us stuck and use them as a clutch? He told me to trust him because he could have shown me better than he could have told me. But was I willing to trust him before it was all manifested?

So, I trusted him to bring him out of the enemy's camp and that is exactly what he did. During it all, I never stopped going to church. I did not stop praising him, I did not stop getting in his word, and I did not stop trusting him. I believed everything that he told me, and it manifested right before my eyes. My son went on to graduate from high school and is now in college, dominating the basketball court. God turned his mess into a message that can change the lives of younger generations to come. Praise God.

Chapter 10
About Time

In March of twenty-one, what started out as a friendship years ago blossomed into a beautiful relationship between myself and my brother in Christ. About time! It took two long years for God to finally bring us together, as I already knew that he would. Now our journey as a Christian couple in pursuit of marriage had begun. As I stated before, I had already known that this man was going to be my husband because God had told me so back in the year two thousand-nineteen. I knew that he loved God and walked in his ways of righteousness because of the fruit that he bore and that made coming alongside him in our season of courtship even better.

The Bible talks about not being unequally yoked with anyone, whether it be a relationship, friendship, or business relationship, because how can two people walk together unless they agree? And the agreeance that both must establish is that Christ is Lord, and we must walk in his ways of righteousness. Here is a little advice: before you get into a relationship with someone make sure that both of you are clear of what one another's intentions and desires are.

Make sure that your spiritual beliefs are the same, with God being the source of all things. Women make sure that God sent that man into your life and men make sure that God led you to that Woman and not your lustful desires. Men are supposed to love their wives like Christ loves the church, and women are supposed to respect their husbands as the priesthood of their homes, and that is what I intended to go by. Getting to know my soon-to-be husband was a joy and a challenge altogether. There, you had two uniquely made individuals trying to come together as one while getting on each other's nerves. I was the quiet, calm, and collected one, while he was the outgoing, outspoken, and friendly one.

It is safe to say that opposites attract because we were night and day in physicality, but God knew what he was doing when he brought us together. Our strengths and weaknesses balanced each other out, but what we both needed spiritually for God's kingdom work had to be imparted to one another. When I first saw this man, we were at a church function, and he was leading prayer for that program. He was so loud. His voice sounded like thunder, as if it were raining on a stormy day. I looked at my cousin and said to her dang, that man is loud, but what caught my attention was the confidence and boldness in the Lord he had.

I was not interested in him at that moment, but the power of God was what I had felt through his prayer. I wanted what he had boldness and confidence from God so that I could be able to do what God called me to do but the only way I was going to have that was through a continued relationship with Christ. This man was bold for God, as he still is today. He was honest and stood on God's truths. He did not mind telling you what God's word said in love. That was so attractive to me.

A man after God's heart was what I had prayed for, and his looks just sweetened the deal. He was very attentive to my wants and needs, and he treated my children as if they were his own. He was a positive role model and an example of what a godly man was supposed to be, but with any new relationship when children are involved, there is a transitional process that must come forth for all sides. There were some bumping heads going back and forth, words being tossed in the air, and bonds that had to be built on God's principles. I was the peacemaker, the quiet one who took everything to God in prayer, the one who smoothed things out, but there were times that the transitioning process into God's order was hard for me, too.

I was so used to being by myself and not having to answer to anyone, but thank God I had a cousin who held me accountable and would tell me the hard, ugly truths about myself. She was there before our courtship began and she is still today. She was not a judgmental person. She always looked at people's points of view with a godly perspective, giving all the benefit of the doubt and speaking God's truth in love no matter who you were. Sometimes, I hated listening to what she told me, but being told the truth allowed me to grow more mature in Christ.

I knew we got on her nerves a lot because she once told us that we were playing with her emotions because of our stubbornness and lack of honesty about our feelings toward each other. In that season of my life, we called ourselves the Three Musketeers. We were always together, learning, growing, healing, and encouraging one another in the Lord.

After all, that is what Christians are supposed to do. But there was still work to be done, and God had his hands full when it came to us. The devil was persistent in trying to stop what God had ordained, but our trust and dependence on Christ was what brought us through. As we continued to grow in love, our relationship grew stronger, and our feelings grew deeper for one another. I had fallen madly in love with that man, but I was not about to tell him that. At that time, he was visiting churches and in pursuit of a church home to call his own because of unforeseen circumstances, but when God led him to our church, he decided to rededicate his life to Christ and become a member. Now, he is the Assistant Pastor there.

To God be the glory for all that he had done. God kept showing up and answering prayers for us. I am a firm believer that everything that God has promised you will come to past if you are obedient unto him and you are committed to doing his will.

Five months had passed and the expected had unexpectedly

happened. On August 22 of that year, we were enjoying a high time in the Lord at church, and I was so happy because a lot of my family members from my dad's side of the family had come to visit that day. There was nothing unusual that day because my family would visit occasionally. I was happy to see them because, at that time I had not seen them for a while. But before the service was over, all the attention shifted towards the front of the church, where I could see my boyfriend standing holding a microphone.

It was not surprising for me to see him standing in front of the church, but when he called my name and asked if I would join him in front of the whole congregation, my suspicious antennas began to go up. I did not know what to expect, but that did not stop me from giving him the side-eye. As I had begun to walk to the front of the church my mind went blank. I could not think of any reason he would have called me up there, but when he glided down on one knee with that clean white suit he had on, I knew exactly what he was about to do. I was shocked.

We had talked about marriage a few times throughout our conversations, but I did not expect it to be that soon. He did his little smooth talk like the poet that he is and sucked me right on in. I melted like putty in his hand as I cried and agreed to take his hand in marriage. Not only were a lot of my family members there, but his mom, daughter, and sister were there, too. His sister was laughing so badly because she knew that I was a big water bag. You know, that is what someone would call you if you were a crybaby, and a crybaby is exactly what I was.

I had so many mixed emotions going on at that time because he knew that I did not like surprises, he knew that I did not like being the center of attention, and he knew that I did not like being filmed, but in the end, none of that really mattered because that man wanted to spend the rest of his life with me. After all that was over, I still gave him and my family an ear full of carefully chosen words. From that day forward, we began to plan our wedding.

I never really knew how much time, effort, and thought was put into a wedding until we started planning our own. Some people normally have at least a year to plan for a wedding, but we had seven months to do it, and boy, was it overwhelming at times. But it was fun being able to put together our own desires of how we wanted our wedding to be, and it turned out to be amazingly beautiful. We danced the night away, but our clothes did not fall off like David's did in the Bible.

Chapter 11
Blessings

The very next morning, we headed out for our honeymoon. Boy, was my husband in for a surprise, so I had thought. We had chosen a secluded romantic place to venture into called Blue Ridge, GA. We had decided to stay in a log cabin but really did not know what we were getting ourselves into. As we viewed the beautiful pictures online together before booking it and arriving there, we were overwhelmed with excitement because we had finally gotten a chance to spend some alone time together, but the roadways we had to drive to get there took the excitement away instantly at that moment.

We were not even thinking about doing what grown people do. Our lives were at stake. There were so many steep hills, valleys, and roadways where neither had guardrails for protection but plenty of drop-offs waiting for us to tumble down. It seemed like we were in one of those scary scenes in a movie where you would see a murderer appear out of nowhere and knock you off a cliff. We were scared out of our minds just from the driving experience alone. Talking about a surprise for my husband, whew, that was a surprise for me, too.

I had never experienced anything like that before. As soon as we had gotten over one steep hill made of dirt there was another one made of gravel. That was a scary situation to be in because while driving on the gravel roadways, our car began to kick up the gravel as if we were moving at a rapid speed, and it did not help that we were driving at night into unknown territories. People were speeding and going around us as if they were in a hurry but, it turns out they were just doing the speed limit. It had just been us driving 10 miles per hour, but thank God, we made it there safely.

When we arrived too the cabin, the first thing that caught our eye was a sign that said do not feed the bears with a bear statue standing right next to it. My husband repeated what was written on the sign as if he were in shock. What he did not know was while I was looking through all the pictures online without him, I had seen pictures of bears that previous guests had posted for the cabin's reviews. In my mind, I was not scared. I wanted to see a bear in person. I do not know what I was thinking, but I did keep that information from him because I knew if he had seen those bears, it would have been a response like this: "Woman, you must be out of your mind. I'm going to have to pull your black card for that." He was so funny.

As we were getting out of the car, pressed together like a peanut butter and jelly sandwich because it was nighttime, we swiftly took cover and hurried to the door of the cabin. That was the longest 5 minutes of my life trying to open the door using the code to get in. My husband was standing behind me, looking around as if there were invaders after us. You would have thought that he was back in the military the way he kept watch. Finally, I managed to get the door open, and we rushed in with no hesitation. We scooped the place out to make sure we were safe and that everything was up to our standards because if it had not been, my husband had made it clear that we would be staying at a hotel for that night. Who was he kidding? I was not about to get back into that car and make another trip down Death Hill. Suffering made sense at that moment because daylight had not come.

My husband then went back outside to get our luggage, and boy, was I a nervous wreck. I looked through the window just to make sure nothing was going to attack him. I yelled babe, are you okay? And the response he had given me had me in tears from laughing at him. He yelled back at me, 'If I was not, what were you going to do?" He was right. What was I going to do? Well, I guess I would have been the one to live to tell the story.

The next day, we awakened to a beautiful sight of God's creation that we could finally see while it was daylight. There was a stream that led to a lake, beautiful tall trees, and other cabins built on stilts. I really did not know what we were thinking when we chose this cabin online. Some things just look better in a picture. Next time we will enjoy the beautiful sight from a distance.

Could you imagine bringing younger children on a trip like that? Our teenage children would have been swinging from the cabin as if they were on monkey bars. That drop-down from the cabin was to die for, and we wanted no part of that. The remainder of our honeymoon was pleasant. The city's view was beautiful, and the people there were kind, but we had little people at home who were missing our presence, so we headed back home.

When we arrived back home, we were met with hugs and kisses from our younger children, of course. The teenagers were not so surprised to see us because they were living their best lives while we were gone. The partying ended, and we got back to reality. It was for them and us. I am a firm believer that when you trust God and lean not to your own understanding, God will blow your mind.

Here I am, living my best life, saved, sanctified, and filled with the Holy Ghost, married with a beautiful family that God has blessed me with all because he loves me. God said he would do exceedingly abundantly above all you can ask or think, and he proved that to be true. He is a man of his word, and they do not return unto him void. He is loving, caring, and faithful, and he wants the best for you. If you can believe God for what he said, then you too can live this fairytale life. All hail to King Jesus for all that he has done for us.

About The Author

84

Shareka Marbra is a devoted woman of God with an unyielding passion to please our Lord and Savior Jesus Christ. She is the author of Jesus Inspired Poems Photos and Songs and a recording artist of 2 gospel songs available on YouTube, as well as the worship leader and minister at her local church where she serves. She is also an entrepreneur as the sole business owner of a non-emergency transportation service for the elderly named Endless Journeys by Shareka Marbra. Mrs. Marbra also holds the title as a Godly wife and awesome mother. She is very close with family and takes joy in making others' lives better. But what she loves most is drawing people to our Lord Jesus Christ salvation